Tough Luck Cookie

You're Getting A Brother

Written and Illustrated By

Andrea Brasier

Copyright © 2019 Andrea Brasier

All rights reserved.

ISBN 13: 978-1-7335762-2-2

Dedication

To my three boys!

Ethan, Matthew, and Gabriel.

Tough luck Cookie, you're getting a brother.

You'll have to share your toys with another.

He's not coming today or even tomorrow.

Wipe off that frown and toss out that sorrow.

He's someone to love and ever so sweet.

Not someone to shove or make smell your feet.

He might cry out at night because he is scared.

But you can help calm him by petting his hair.

He might chew on your toys .

He might even slobber.

Just give him a chance, don't give him a clobber.

You'll grow to love him, just wait and see.

Have patience and kindness, for that is the key.

## About the Author and Illustrator

Andrea Brasier is a wife and mom of three sons. She grew up with parents in the military and lived with one toe in the United States and the other in Germany. Georgia is home to her. Andrea has her BFA in Art Education from Georgia State University in Atlanta, Ga. She loves drawing, painting, writing stories, reading, and so much more. She loves Jesus and without him, none of this journey would be possible at all.

All artwork was created with Copic Markers on Strathmore Marker Paper by Andrea Brasier.

You can see more art by Andrea on Facebook: Drawn To Paint

Color with Cookie!

Enjoy these next few pages by coloring in Cookie with crayons, markers, colored pencils, etc.

www.ingramcontent.com/pod-product-compliance
Lightning Source LLC
LaVergne TN
LVHW072117070426
835510LV00002B/93